Shayla & Friends

Barchelle Bolger Wathen
@shaylaandfriends.com

Copyright © 2022 Barchelle Bolger Wathen

All rights reserved. No part of this book may be used or reproduced in any manner whatsoever without written permission except in the case of brief quotations embodied in critical articles and reviews.

Printed in the United States of America

Paperback ISBN: 978-1-64873-298-0
eBook ISBN: 978-1-64873-299-7

Dedication

This true story is dedicated to the inspiration of the Korniyko family, Mykola Yuhimenko, and the other children of OTCHIY DIM (aka FATHER'S HOUSE), a Christian orphanage in Ukraine (temporarily in Germany), and their supporters like Bruce Elliott, who helped Shayla find her forever family in America.

Roman Korniyko and his family show such beautiful Christian love, dedication, and self-sacrifice to all in their care. They raised Shayla (and many other dogs), in addition to the children, with such incredible commitment and care they deserve. I was honored to meet Roman and Bruce when they brought Shayla to America. Roman and Father's House represent the strength of Ukraine and its people, and God's faithfulness.

It is also dedicated to the animals lost and abandoned in Ukraine because of the war, such as the dog Nala of Father's House. Lost but never forgotten.

Table of Contents

Dedication..*i*

Chapter One: Early Days – Blaze & Riley 1

Chapter Two: Alaskan Shepherd Sweet Juneau 11

Chapter Three: Let the Adventure Begin 19

Chapter Four: What is a German Shepherd/Czechoslovakian Wolfdog? 26

Chapter Five: God's Plan (Father's House)................32

Chapter Six: Young Shayla in Ukraine......................39

Chapter Seven: A Fond Farewell to Ukraine 48

Chapter Eight: Crossing the Bridge to America 55

Chapter Nine: Shayla's New Life...............................64

Chapter Ten: Moving On Together..........................71

Chapter Eleven: Shayla's Future Plans.....................82

Epilogue: Follow Up With Father's House..................89

Acknowledgments..98

Author's Bio..101

Other works by Barchelle...102

References...103

There is a special place in Ukraine called Otchiy Dim (aka Father's House), where all orphaned young, children and pets alike, are loved, embraced, and accepted for the precious lives they are. Roman Korniyko, his wife, daughters Anastasia and Alina, and many others, have dedicated their lives to caring for these precious souls. Roman gave up his medical career and dream of becoming the youngest professor in his medical field to establish this charity home for homeless, orphaned children and pets. Through uncertain times of change and adversity, lack of finances, and dangerous political unrest, Roman bravely followed God's direction. True happiness comes in following God's path of love.

As the verse Joshua 1:9 in the Bible states:

"Have I not commanded you? Be strong and courageous. Do not be afraid; do not be discouraged, for the Lord your God will be with you wherever you go."

Shayla's life also exemplifies this verse – strength, courage, and faith. The remarkable life of the young dog Shayla (originally named Layla) began in this special place. She was born in Ukraine and raised at Father's House, just outside of Kiev, by the Korniyko family and a young orphaned boy named Mykola Yuhimenko.

Together, Mykola and Shayla shared the loneliness of abandonment at an early age, strengthened by the love and friendship of an adoptive Father's House family and God's constant presence.

*Love will find you
When you need it most.
When you're scared
Listen with your soul,
Hear Love call you forth
Even across the oceans.*
By Barchelle (Chelly) Bolger Wathen

Chapter One:
Early Days – Blaze & Riley

Shayla's story begins in Ukraine. However, this story begins long before I knew of Ukraine, Father's House, or sweet Shayla. My life began across the world, in California, in America. In the end, God directed our paths to intertwine.

As the daughter of two Minnesota farm kids, I grew up loving animals with passion, especially dogs. Although my two older brothers, Bruce and Barry, and I grew up in suburban San Diego instead of a lively farm, our family never failed to include at least one dog and a cat or two. My childhood love of animals carried on into adulthood.

Our family dogs included Bokie the beagle (got to love that beagle bay), Fritz the German Shepherd (formerly owned by a police officer), then finally Riska our fluffy, sweet Elk-Kee (Norwegian elkhound/keeshond mix - the rarer and more exotic the dog, the better).

My brothers left for college in Los Angeles while I was just in my first year of junior high school, so I felt more like an only child as a teenager. As a shy daughter of a stern substitute teacher, with braces and poor athletic skills, I was not the most popular kid in school. So I selected only a few close friends to trust.

I was blessed with a wonderful father, Herbert Bolger, who was my hero as a young child and my trusted friend and advisor as an adult. He was a favorite high school counselor who helped so many young students find their way in life. He guided his students, my brothers, and me, with wisdom and patience. Sometimes when we were out together, a prior student stopped to say hello and tell me what a positive difference he made in their lives. Some students he inspired to pursue great careers, and some he walked with through a dark time when they thought of suicide. I was so proud of him; to be blessed with the love and devotion of a good father. I recognized those qualities in God (and later in Roman). He passed on when I was only 30, and my world never truly felt complete again.

I am empathetic, especially for young kids who did not grow up with a loving father. Following his example, as an adult I joined the Big Sister League and was matched with a few young gals as a mentor. My first little sister Crystal ("Kristie") and I are still "sisters" today, over 30 years later.

My mother Shirlee Bolger and I did not always agree when I was a child. Later in life, I realized that her dramatic flair and on-stage persona as an opera chorister/church soloist and teacher had inspired me. She was a great example to help me overcome my shyness and enjoy social interactions more. I busied myself with work, friends, and community and volunteer activities, even as a church soloist. Eventually, I learned the beauty of "Be still and know that I am God," and taking the time to balance my life and to listen to God.

Besides my wonderful dad, our dogs were sometimes my favorite companions and best friends. Going away to college was the best of times (learning and living on campus with my friends), but occasionally the worst of times (living away from home without my canine companions). After college, I remained in San Diego, close to my parents and home.

At church, I met a wonderful guy named Buzzy. He was my age, but had accomplished so much, despite having Cystic Fibrosis. He had grown up strong on his grandfather's cattle ranch, but was now pursuing his master's degree in genetic research in San Diego, researching a cure for his disease. He had such a keen sense of humor and was always happy, despite his condition. Buzzy was my best friend, and like my third brother. He was brilliant, and a few years after he died of his illness, he was awarded his sought-after degree posthumously, based on his extensive research. He made such a difference in his profession. But most of all, I missed my kind, wise, and caring best friend. He taught me to look beyond a person's physical condition, to cherish each precious moment we shared, and to love a man as a dear friend. His motto was "I loved my ever- expanding universe, and those who roamed it with me."

While working as a bookkeeper in a locksmith shop, I met a creative artist/locksmith named Mike. We worked together and became good friends. After he left our shop for another job, we started dating. Eventually, after a rocky relationship, we married. He already had two young sons when we met, so we became an instant family in one home. We were not blessed with children together, so I bargained, pleaded, and whined (a lot) to adopt a pet to complete our chaotic family. Not just any pet, but a young puppy who could grow up with the boys (okay, and fulfill that nurturing side of me).

Our first dog Blaze was a two-month-old black Labrador retriever puppy with a blaze of white across his chest. He was a little rascal, chewing my shoes, Bible, our chaise lounge pad, and the boys' socks, but oh so precious.

When Blaze was a couple of years old, Mike and I went on a trip with friends. We discussed finding a companion dog for Blaze as he grew older. As fate took over, one morning we woke up at the hotel to hear a puppy crying nearby. Mike went outside to investigate and came back awhile later with the cutest little reddish-brown and black puppy following behind him. The little pup came over and cuddled up beside me. Not a word was said, just a nodding glance between Mike and I to say, "Yes, this is the one." God blessed us with that little guy, I just did not yet know how important he would become in my life. We attended an event nearby at a place called Riley's Farm, so it seemed fitting to name him Riley. Turned out that the prior night little Riley got his head stuck between the gateposts to the hotel swimming pool, trying to get a drink of water. He had no tag, and hotel staff told Mike they saw someone dump him out of a car early that morning. We loved him from the moment we met him.

We took Riley home and introduced him to Blaze, who barked at him to establish he was lead dog. Then they were usually inseparable from that day on. A visit to our vet confirmed he was in good health and determined he was a German Shepherd/Australian cattle dog mix. Riley became my best friend, protector, confidante, and truly my canine soulmate.

Over the next several years, Mike's sons grew up with their own lives and interests. Mike and I grew apart as I watched him destroy his/our life as an active alcoholic. I was very sad, because Mike had been the love of my life and best friend over the prior decade. I felt rejected and abandoned. My increasingly sad, lonely days were alleviated thanks to God, my work, and MY boys Blaze and Riley.

When Mike and I finally divorced, I remained in our home, alone except for my faithful canines. In those days, I just went through the motions of everyday life. Caring for my dogs gave me purpose, structure, and strength to rise and face each new morning. Through those tough times I endured to find my own strength and faith in God. To supplement my income, I took in a couple of roommates and got involved with friends and family, church and volunteering with local dog rescues. Together with Blaze and Riley, I endured, finding each day a little more peaceful and happier.

Eventually, I met my second husband George through our church. What a couple – George tall at 6'1", slender with blonde hair, and I am short at 5'2" and slender with dark brown hair. Opposites attract but we complement each other's strengths in many ways. He was a self-employed landscaper, supervising and running his own business, while I was entrenched in the stability of government bureaucracy as a San Diego City Attorney paralegal for decades. He is so technically and mechanically gifted, while my strength is in scholastics and administrative work. He is content to be at home, a constant in my life, while I am always ready to seek out the next adventure. He grounds and balances my life when I fly too high (I love those ziplines). He is also my hero as he has overcome so many obstacles such as a major car accident as a young man that caused numerous health issues, and diabetes. He has always been a very hardworking man, and always strives to overcome setbacks. We became good friends through sharing church singles group activities, and a few slow country dances. He was not yet an avid dog lover, but he learned that the way to my heart meant accepting Riley and Blaze as an essential part of my life.

The three of us grew on him as we married and became a family. Not only was I blessed and happy again, but the dogs found a fun companion in George, who would play with them, chasing them through the house. One of Blaze's favorite times involved George swinging a rope toy in the air as Blaze hung on tight on the other end, feet in mid-air. George and I did not have any children, so our dogs became our "fur kids."

As the years passed, the dogs aged, lost their energy, developed cancerous growths, and we knew it was time to let them go. We could not let them suffer. We called their veterinarian who scheduled a date to come over to our home and arrange a peaceful end for both of them. The previous night, we had a farewell gathering for Blaze and Riley with our family and friends who also loved them, Mike, and our pastor who blessed them. I spent our last night together holding them, telling them what good dogs they were, and thanking them for their love and friendship, especially Riley.

When the vet came over the next day, the dogs passed away on their beds on our patio, in our arms, as we told them how much we loved them.

I played one of my favorite Celine Dion's songs "Fly" in the background. *"Fly, fly precious one. Your endless journey has begun. Take your gentle happiness, far too beautiful for this. Cross over to the other shore. There is peace forevermore."*

A gentle breeze stirred on the still, hot July day, blowing the wind chimes that bore their names. So quickly, MY boys, and a key chapter of my life with Mike, were gone. What would I do now that my favorite role as "Super Dog Mom" was completed? Once the vet had taken their bodies away and everyone left, I sat alone in the backyard crying. Suddenly two beautiful reddish butterflies flew past me, and I knew God took their spirits, they were safe with Him forevermore. A piece of my heart and soul went with them.

Chapter Two:
Alaskan Shepherd Sweet Juneau

Over the next couple of months, the silence in our empty home, without our dogs, grew deafening. It seemed that even the neighborhood cats sensed our emotional loss and started hanging out in our driveway to get attention. Their presence made me smile for a short time, despite the pain. I tried to continue my daily walks, only to break into tears when I saw a person with their dog. I continued to volunteer at the San Diego Humane Society and even completed the Animal Law Enforcement Academy training. Many of the rescue dogs I volunteered with touched my heart (like sweet Shepherd Boltan). But George knew I would not be happy without our own dog to love, so he suggested we start looking for another companion. We knew we could never replace those dear friends, especially Riley. But we also knew our hearts were big enough to love again and give a dog that needed a loving home a chance at a good life. George wanted to experience raising a dog from a puppy, and I agreed, although I remembered only too well how much work puppies require.

Not long after, we found an ad for a German Shepherd/Alaskan Malamute puppy named "Ritz." He was at a local animal shelter. We met him within a few days, just in time before other people wanted to adopt him. We later renamed him "Juneau" after the capitol of Alaska (a good name for an Alaskan Malamute).

Juneau was one of three brothers. Initially they lived as scared puppies in an abusive and unhappy home, then were shuttled through a series of rescue shelters in California. We met all three puppies, but chose to adopt Juneau as the bravest of the shy siblings. Although I volunteered with San Diego Humane Society and other animal organizations for many years, I had never seen such sad, dejected little pups. Beautiful long-haired furballs, smart, but painfully shy. Juneau had a great trainer, Rob Kuty, at the rescue shelter, who helped encourage him before we met. Rob taught us how to work with him and bolster his confidence. Rob worked with zoo and stage animals and knew dogs well. He had such a great relationship with Juneau that even after we adopted this special pup, Rob came to our home to see him. Juneau still ran to leap into his arms. Later on, Rob also trained Juneau on agility coursework.

But despite the training he received, Juneau would still jump at any little noise and shy away from people's touch (even ours at first). He often walked with his tail down between his legs in any new situation. His brother Hilton was even returned to the shelter three times because he was so shy. We were glad to adopt Juneau and take him to a stable home life. When we took this little guy to a dog park, he would run away from any dogs fighting or getting too close and personal. Though he liked to run with the big dogs and make them chase him (he ran so fast as a young pup), if they got too close, he would jump on top of a nearby picnic table or tree log for safety; just enough to tease the other dogs, but avoid any trouble.

A couple of years later, we adopted a yellow Labrador retriever, Honey, on the recommendation that a braver older female may help Juneau come out of his shell in a way that nobody else could. She was already six years old when we brought her home. We looked at several other dogs, but she was Juneau's choice. She was outgoing, brave, comical, and confident, with an oversized personality. Honey became Juneau's playmate, teacher, and encourager. She was my comedian and confidante. Some of her favorite activities included jumping up to catch the water as it flowed out of the hose, and diving into a grove of trees to catch her favorite tennis ball. By watching and following her lead, Juneau blossomed into a playful and happy dog. They bonded quickly as companions and loved being together, even when he chased then ran away from her, always just out of her reach.

But again, as happens with all good relationships, the years went by all too quickly. Despite veterinarian care and lots of love, sweet Honey died from a stroke at age 13. She spent her last couple of weeks growing feeble to the point where she could not walk or enjoy life. But we were not the only ones to feel her loss. Our gentle, shy Juneau seemed so lost and alone without his "big sister." From the first night we brought Honey home and Juneau slept beside her crate, to the last night as our aging girl could barely move from her crate bed, he would not leave her side. They were forever friends.

The night after we returned home from the vet's office without our girl, Juneau laid right beside that same crate, now void and quiet, with his head on her blanket. Surely, he also missed her and understood our tears. But I think he also celebrated her spirit, knowing her soul would live on.

Over the next couple of months, we all went through the motions of life, quietly. George was busy working as a landscaper, gone most days. I worked now as a Senior Paralegal with the City Attorney (almost a 30- year career).

Like so many others, I primarily worked from home in those initial post-COVID months. That change made Honey's loss more poignant, as I had once worked from home with my two sidekick canine co-workers laying at my side, ready for a quick hug or ball toss at any moment.

Prior to those COVID days, I came home from working all day to study, research, and write papers for my master's degree online, often late into the night and on weekends. Juneau and Honey were my constant companions and encouragers, listening to my rantings over one too many assignments and exams, or to my supposed brilliant research papers proofread aloud, ever ready to disturb the silence with a good playtime chase and barking contest.

They were both there to console George and I when my mom, my last parent, died. Becoming an orphan, even as an adult, was such a difficult life transition. I felt abandoned, lonely, jealous of other people who could casually talk about calling their parents and sharing activities, and even frustrated with people who did not spend time with their aging parents. I would have given anything for just one more day with my parents. Now I felt lost in a world where I could no longer "call home" and I was forevermore the responsible adult. My childhood was truly over.

Now Juneau lay alone, grateful for the moments I could break away from working at the computer, or George would come home from work and just pet him. Once again, our home seemed especially quiet and empty without Honey's sunshine. Would we love and adopt another dog again?

Chapter Three:
Let the Adventure Begin

As my volunteer work with a few local dog rescue groups continued, I checked local pet rescue computer ads, secretly looking for the next dog who might complete our family again. I was certain Juneau also needed a fun and courageous companion again. However, I was nervous to admit to George that I wanted another canine companion. But I think he knew that.

George loves dogs more than he will sometimes admit, but he needs time to accept and agree to new ideas and adventures, especially if they involve extra cost or work. But I gradually encouraged the idea of another dog and gave him time to realize how much we ALL needed to take that next step again.

Over the next couple of months, we continued to search the shelter ads and even met a few dogs at some local shelters. Juneau accompanied us to meet the dogs, but none of them seemed a good match for him. We even adopted a dog for a few weeks from one of the shelters where I volunteered – a white German Shepherd. Unfortunately, that dog was just plain OCD-crazy, chasing and growling at his tail violently, throwing up whenever he got in a moving vehicle, growling at his food, and trying to bite Juneau twice for attempting to play. Finally, Juneau ended up hiding out in the back room to avoid this dog. Not at all the buddy we wanted for our sweet boy, or the fun, loving companion that we wanted. He went back to the rescue and was adopted by a single woman with no other pets, a great match.

Then one day we saw that perfect ad – a young, female German Shepherd mix named Layla (we later renamed her Shayla). Amazing Strays Rescue was the posting rescue group. The ad stated Layla liked other dogs, outings, and was in good health. Her pictures were beautiful. Of course, we were a bit biased because she looked like she could have been Juneau's younger cousin, both black and tan beautiful Shepherd mixes. Was this an answer to our prayers?

Her profile sounded good, even George agreed. So, I submitted the online application and waited to hear back, silently praying for God to let this be our "right" dog. One magical night in November 2020, I got that call I will never forget from one of the rescue volunteers, Sarah. She told me the rescue received several applications for Layla, but mine stood out because I already had a lot of experience as a dog volunteer and a German Shepherd owner. It seemed like God answered our prayers.

I asked if the three of us (Juneau included, of course) could meet this dog, as we wanted to ensure a good match for Juneau. Then I learned the rest of the story – this dog was not actually in San Diego, or even in America, and Sarah had never met the dog. Wait - WHAT???

Sarah explained that her father, Bruce Elliott, a San Diego businessman, was a long-term board member, co-founder, and supporter of Father's House. He and others had been involved in rescuing at least 15 dogs already and transporting them from Ukraine to California. WOW – our potential new dog lived in another country that we knew almost nothing about! Layla (Shayla) and a few other dogs were certified in good health by a veterinarian in Ukraine, had passports, and would be coming to America later that November. Geesh, George and I did not even have passports then.

The volunteer described her as good with other dogs, even helping to raise litters of puppies at the orphanage. Although she could be dominant (wouldn't that describe most alpha female dogs?), she might be a good match with easygoing Juneau. Sarah told me that another family previously adopted a similar looking dog from the orphanage and ran a DNA test which indicated the dog was a Shepherd/Czechoslovakian Wolfdog. Shayla could be the same breed. She asked if I was still interested.

Again, WOW! God seemed to have a sense of humor in answering our prayers. George and I discussed this, as we had never heard of this breed before. I will admit our first thought was that "wolfdog" sounded a bit intimidating. But as I said earlier about my childhood dog Riska, the rarer and exotic the dog, the better. The only knowledge I had then was that dogs descended from wolves at some point in their evolution. Without hesitation,

I told Sarah, "YES we want her."

I knew about German Shepherds, but now I set out to learn about Czechoslovakian Wolfdogs and what we had just agreed to adopt!

About a week or two later, Sarah called me back to say Shayla and the other dogs should arrive in San Diego around Thanksgiving.

One last question: "Will you be ready, and are you still interested?"

We said, "Absolutely, provided Juneau approves of her upon meeting."

Our world was about to change forever, in ways we had never dreamed - a culture and world so foreign to us, but one we would come to genuinely love.

For a couple that never had kids, our hearts were about to embrace an entire orphanage family. We even became sponsors for a young child at Father's House. Let the adventure begin, trusting God!

Chapter Four:
What is a German Shepherd/Czechoslovakian Wolfdog?

Before Shayla's arrival, I researched all I could find about Czechoslovakian Wolfdogs and wolfdog/German Shepherd mixes. I read that the Czechoslovakian Wolfdog (aka Vlcak) is a distinctively attractive and larger breed, most notable for its wolf-like appearance, especially the head, face, and tail. The breed has superior eyesight/hearing/sense of smell. Such dogs are protective and loyal to family, and okay with other dogs. These canines are highly energetic and alert to all around them, muscular and athletic, and known for endurance. They have a relatively long lifespan, about 15 years. (YAY!!)

They can be good companions for active owners who enjoy outdoor activities, though not recommended for first-time dog owners and families with small children. (Well, that might be wolfdogs who did not grow up in orphanages surrounded by children, like Shayla.) No wonder Sarah liked my previous experience with German Shepherds and numerous breeds as a dog rescue volunteer.

The Czechoslovakian Vlcak is a primitive breed of dog with a dominant and independent spirit, needing consistency and patience. This dog is confident, lively, active, and obedient, with quick reactions. They are also highly intelligent, versatile, and curious.

The American Kennel Club emphasized, "Early socialization and training is important."

Since Shayla grew up at Father's House with many other dogs, cats, kids, and adults, we knew she possessed early socialization skills. Plus, the German Shepherd dog is usually good with children. But she had never been formally trained; that would be up to us. Fortunately, we already had years of dog training experience, thanks to Rob and my San Diego Humane Society trainers!

The Vlcak breed was originally bred for border patrol in Czechoslovakia in the 1950s, due to interbreeding involving German Shepherd dogs and Carpathian wolves (smaller than timber and gray wolves). This interbreeding resulted in a working dog with improved health and stamina, longer lifespans, and increased keen senses and intelligence, without the health problems common in many modern dog breeds. The offspring were used as military and patrol dogs. They are currently used in Europe and the United States for search and rescue, tracking, obedience, agility, drafting, herding, and working dog sports, as well as companions.

In 1982, the Czechoslovakian Kennel Club[1] granted full recognition to the Czechoslovakian Wolfdog and named it a national breed. While it is a fairly popular breed in Eastern Europe and Russia, the Czechoslovakian Wolfdog remained a relatively unknown breed in America until the last couple of decades. In 2001, the American Kennel Club (AKC)[2] entered the breed into its Foundation Stock Service (AKC-FSS) under the name Czechoslovakian Vlcak, the first step towards full recognition in that organization. In 2006, the United Kennel Club (UKC) granted full recognition to the Czechoslovakian Wolfdog as a member of the Herding Dog Group. In 2009, the breed earned its first UKC Championship Title, and in 2010, the breed was eligible to compete in AKC Companion Dog events.

I also learned that a raw diet is preferable for the Czechoslovakian Vlcak, but high-quality, grain-free kibble with raw supplements is also acceptable. Perfect, I had already seen the benefits of such a diet with Riley, who returned from serious illness once he started eating more natural food with supplements. Just one more step to

---

[1] (Club, n.d.)
[2] (America, n.d.)

transition to a raw diet. Over the years, both Shayla and old boy, Juneau, have done well on a much more natural and often raw diet.

Mixed with German Shepherd breed traits of high intelligence, loyalty, confidence, plus a steady and courageous demeanor, we felt confident Shayla would be a good match for us.

Chapter Five:
God's Plan
(Father's House)

Roman Korniyko & Bruce Elliott

As our lives continued in America, we had no idea that a cute, perky shepherd puppy was growing up at an orphanage in Ukraine. The information on Shayla's early days was provided by her early caretakers and companions, the Korniyko family and Mykola of Father's House, along with Bruce Elliott. Together Roman, his family, and Bruce helped Shayla, and at least 16 other dogs, safely journey to forever homes in America (and one to Germany).

To fully understand Shayla's story with Father's House, I must first tell their story. Roman Korniyko was a promising young medical doctor in Ukraine, married and father of two daughters, Anastasia and Alina. His journey to create Otchiy Dim (Father's House) began 25 years ago, when God answered his fervent prayers to restore his failing marriage and family happiness. He prayed that his daughters would not grow up without their father. To show his thanks, he offered his heart and service to God, who opened his eyes to see the homeless in Ukraine. He never imagined leaving his medical career to work with orphans and homeless kids. But when God poured His love into Roman's heart for these children and the Ukrainian people, his life was forever changed. Roman gave up his dream to become the youngest medical professor in his country, but with a grateful heart that God chose him to serve His children.

As Roman has said, "Whatever you dedicate your life to for Jesus is eternal, and you take that with you into eternity. Discover what that purpose is for you, and follow the value in that."

Worldly possessions and dreams will never bring you the degree of happiness that following God's path can provide. If you pursue God's plan with your whole heart, God will provide the miracles to fulfill the dream. Roman's new mission was to be a father to the fatherless, to give these children hope and a future, instead of the trauma and betrayal they had known within their families.

In the early 1990s, Ukraine declared independence from the Soviet Union. The economy was in dire crisis with high unemployment and political corruption, intertwined with high statistics of alcoholism, drug addiction, abuse, and certain depression. Bandits often raided homes, with parents killed and children left orphaned. Two percent of Ukraine's kids were orphans, left alone to run the streets in gangs, begging for food scraps.

Roman started venturing into his local community

to see first-hand the appalling conditions and communicate with the kids who invited him to see where they lived. Their "homes" were often open basements with cast-off mattresses and household items, underground communities with no family or parental support. He saw where the kids would punch holes in the underground water pipes for a trickle of water to shower.

He began to invite a few of these orphans to his home to wash, get clean clothes and food, and spend the night. Although he was nervous to see the orphans stay over and play with his daughters, he was confident God would protect his family's health. God proved faithful, and his daughters were never sick. Initially, he had a 2-bedroom apartment (1 bedroom plus a living room) with 10 orphans joining his family. Then he rented out a second small apartment with 18 kids.

Roman told of a time that police broke into the Korniyko apartment to arrest a boy wanted by juvenile police. The minor offered to give himself up, and by a miracle, the police officer pleaded to the judge to let the boy complete community service rather than face arrest. The officer took Roman before the town's mayor and said "These are the people who change children's lives." The mayor offered to provide a much larger facility, and Otchiy Dim took in up to 30+ orphans.

Although Roman and his family had little money and resources, he began this ministry to the orphans. After three days of fasting and prayer, God provided another miracle. A friend called to say that a lady's mother had passed and left money to be used for charity, and offered Roman those funds to buy a large home for the children. The funds were exactly the value of the home they wanted to buy, their current "blue house" home in Ukraine. Badly in need of restoration, it served as a home where they could all live together. Father's House continued to grow and expand services, providing invaluable charitable service within their community – for homeless children, seniors, and even animals.

The Father's House Christian ministry team, under Roman's direction and his family, created a series of programs designed to create a path to societal integration for the kids. Instead of cold institutions, a home was built, based on a positive family-oriented structure, rehabilitation, and teaching the children their value in society. "To help a parentless child is to restore a generation, unlock the future, and influence history" (per Otchiy Dim website). Finally, the children had "parents" and teachers to exemplify to them the goodness of a family and to teach them about God's love and protection. The Ukrainian economy was starting to improve then, and the people were proud, resilient, and educated.

Father's House has received numerous awards as a foundation for social reform in Ukraine. The orphanage attracted the attention and support of numerous churches and humanitarian service groups. One such group is Ezra International Ukraine, a Christian non-profit that rescues and restores abused, neglected, or abandoned children in that country. Bruce Elliott is Chairman of the Ezra International Father's House Board and Director of Ezra International Ukraine Children's Work. Bruce and his wife Anne became staunch supporters and friends of Roman over 20 years ago, assisting in the rescue of children and animals.

Chapter Six:
Young Shayla in Ukraine

Shayla was found as a young stray puppy, lost and alone on the streets in the village of Petrivske, Kyiv-Svyatoshinsky district (a rural area about an hour south of Kiev), in Ukraine. Amidst the country's economic and humanitarian issues, the life of one puppy may seem insignificant. But Shayla embodies the strength, hope, and resilience of the Ukrainian people.

The streets were a scary, lonely world for a puppy. They were filled with loud cars, bigger mean dogs, and people who had no time for a stray puppy. She survived on whatever scarce food and water she could find. Although an attractive black and tan puppy with a cute white tail tip, she could not compete with so many stray dogs and homeless people for scarce food and attention. She was just another stray, one more problem to most people.

She befriended a young Ukrainian boy named Mykola Yuhimenko. At first, Shayla was fearful of people and trusted no one. Mykola also lost his family at a young age and was alone in the world. He understood her. God brought these two lives together, and Mykola instantly fell in love with Shayla. They quickly bonded and became inseparable, based on their common abandonment and loving hearts. Mykola lived and worked at the Christian orphanage "Father's House" and knew Roman and his adult daughters Alina and Anastasia welcomed homeless dogs as companions for the orphaned children.

Mykola took Shayla to Father's House orphanage, a tall blue building with lots of carefree animals painted over it. Indeed, the Korniyko family welcomed Shayla to live with them, the children, and the other animals.

As she grew up, she found a safe home there. Shayla loved to play with the children whenever she could, games of chasing the ball and running about the yard together. Her love no doubt helped the children, just as they helped her. She was rarely without companionship, as often a little child's hand reached out to pet her soft fur. One of her favorite activities was to roll over as the kids scratched her white tummy. Sometimes one of the children would fall asleep curled up with Shayla, leaving them both feeling safe, strong, and loved. She could be described as "lean and long" as she was slender and stood almost as tall as some of the younger children.

Shayla enjoyed being their companion and quickly learned to love Roman's family and the children, just like Mykola. Over the next few months at Father's House, Alina cared for Shayla and provided whatever food she could. Alina taught Shayla to raise her right paw when she said "Day Lapu" (a greeting meaning something like "give me your paw"), and praised her as a very smart dog. Shayla eventually found purpose in the orphanage by assisting Alina as the lead dog in raising and training the young puppies on how to behave properly.

Some days Mykola would take her out for playful walks, other times they would sit together, and he would open his heart to confide how he was also an orphan. One of the first things he learned at Father's House was how much God loved and accepted him. Father Roman also encouraged him to be good and care about others, taught him skills, and provided for his needs. Although he missed having a forever family, Roman became like a father to Mykola and so many other children.

As a wolfdog, Shayla's instinctual spirit makes her wary of trusting people. She wanted to teach and educate her new Ukrainian family on how to treat her with respect, and occasionally she needed to roam independently on an adventure. There were other dogs here too, of all sizes, and even some cats who would play with her. She seemed to enjoy making friends with all of them, regardless of age, size, personality, disability, or even species, and she learned to accept others just as they are. This was something I learned with my dear friend Buzzy.

Sometimes another dog, Lizze, would join Shayla in bolting and running through the fields into town, carefree and wild, chasing lizards and rabbits along the way, just exploring the boundaries of their world. The dogs learned which strangers in town might be kind to them, and offer some scraps of food. However, the dogs knew that the one place that guaranteed safety was Father's House.

They always returned home to the orphanage, where they might get scolded a bit and not be allowed to run free again for a while. But the moments of roaming free through the village made any scolding from someone at the orphanage worthwhile. Alina and Anastasia would laugh at their determined carefree spirits, hug them, and welcome them home. Surely God does the same when we wander away from Him, but He welcomes us back gladly.

Life was much better at Father's House, although not always easy. Shayla was no longer free to wander whenever she chose. When nobody had time to spend with the dogs, they were tied up or locked into a small fenced enclosure for their safety, sometimes for many hours. They were not allowed to go outside the enclosure to even go potty. Food was scarce at times, limited to scraps and tiny bites. Those were some difficult days. That is why Bruce, Roman, and his family wanted to "rescue" the dogs and bring them to America - to find loving, forever homes of their own as companion pets.

Alina & Shayla

Mykola & Shayla

The Children & Shayla

Chapter Seven:
A Fond Farewell to Ukraine

As Shayla matured into an adult dog and learned to feel safe and loved, her heart healed and grew stronger. Always alert and attentive to her surroundings, she watched as some children and other dogs left with strangers. Her canine friends would never return, but they seemed happy to go. She must have wondered where they went, and if she would leave Father's House one day.

Roman told Shayla once, "One day a forever family will come for you sweet girl, just be patient and wait on God's timing."

Yet the months and years went by, and she could have begun to doubt Roman's promise of her own family. She had to learn to have the patience to wait for the next step in her life, in God's timing.

Then one magical day, her life was to change again. Alina spoke to Shayla and Lizze and a couple of other dogs there to tell them that they were going to leave Father's House and go on a long journey with Roman and Bruce. Finally, these dogs were going to be adopted into their own forever families and homes in America!

Mykola came by to see Shayla and told her, "Your scars and sad times have made you strong little one. You never gave up. Now it is time to find that courage within to be brave and move ahead. I will miss you so much, but I love you more - enough to let you go to a better life with a forever family who can give you everything that I cannot. Thank you for your friendship and companionship. Once the best gift we could give you was safety and security, but now the best gift we can give you is your freedom. Be courageous."

Alina told her, "I will miss you sweet girl, but we love you so much that we want what is best for you. One day you will understand. Be happy, your time has finally come to join your forever family."

In the next couple of weeks, Roman took the dogs to the veterinarian to conduct health exams and obtain the dogs' passports. Early one morning in November 2020, many of the children and Mykola visited the dogs one last time. Hugging the dogs tight, tears fell, and they were speechless as though they could not find the right words to say. Shayla tried to lick the sweet salty tears from Mykola's face and nuzzled her head under his arm, attempting again to comfort her friend. Alina came and sat down beside Shayla as she stretched out across her lap, lying on her back with her legs up in the air to receive one more tummy scratch.

Then Alina and Roman led each dog into a hard crate with a soft blanket and asked them to lie inside. The dogs must have wondered what was happening, but they had learned to trust their handlers. They loaded the dog crates into a large van and headed to the airport. Shayla was always eager for an adventure and to explore new things, but she seemed confused as to where they were going. Before she had too much time to think about it, they arrived at the airport.

The dog crates were rolled away and placed onto the conveyor belt to load them into the plane's cargo hold. This was a cold, dark space with lots of luggage, and the dogs were likely scared. They were not given sedatives or medications to make them sleepy, for fear they could risk heart and respiratory problems alone in the pressurized aircraft. Each time the plane hit an air pocket, moved up or down unexpectedly, or the dogs heard a noise, they likely wondered what was happening. This was a whirlwind of movement for the animals, with everything changing in their world so quickly. The dogs were cramped in their crates without food, and Shayla was unable to stretch out her long legs or comfortably sleep for long. It was a long, quiet, 13-hour flight from Ukraine to Los Angeles, California.

But the last thing Roman had told Shayla was "You will be okay, girl. Just go to sleep for a while, then you will wake up in a new and safer place."

She had always trusted Father Roman. Although she was separated from the only home and friends she knew, she was never separated from God's protection and love. Neither are we, no matter the situation.

"Father" Roman Korniyko

Shayla & Friends in Ukraine

Chapter Eight:
Crossing the Bridge to America

When Shayla woke up, she was in a very different place, with people in uniforms speaking a different language. Her dog friends in their crates were there with her, but she likely wondered where Alina and Mykola, and her children, were. As Mykola said, she gathered her inner courage for the adventure ahead. Soon, though, she joined a happy chorus of barking with her friends as they saw their familiar friends Roman and Bruce there to greet them.

Eventually Bruce and Roman led the dogs outside to the parking lot, into the dark moonless night of Los Angeles, California. Even the air here smelled different, and there were many more lights and people. After the long plane ride and waiting in the airport office, the dogs beelined for a quick potty break and a chance to stretch their legs. Then they were placed back into vans for a long drive to Bruce's home in San Diego. That would be Shayla's first night sleeping inside a real home.

The next day, Bruce, his wife, and Roman woke up the sleepy dogs for a yummy breakfast and a short walk, before getting into Bruce's car. Shayla spied the open front passenger seat right next to Bruce. She assumed it must be open for her, so she jumped up in front, better to see the world from there. Roman looked in the car and laughed, and graciously got into the back seat. Okay, Shayla was ready for an adventure. They drove out to the countryside (to Lakeside), and came to our large ranch house with a large open field and many trees, fenced in on all sides, peaceful and quiet.

George and I were busy that morning, setting up her dog crate with soft blankets, toys, a bag of treats, and even a sign to say "Welcome Home Shayla" (officially changing her name from Layla to Shayla). Juneau got a bath that morning and was sporting a new blue collar, just like Shayla's new pink collar. We anxiously awaited our new friends, and although I'm not sure Juneau knew what to expect, he seemed to share in our excitement. After a long month of waiting and wondering about a dog we had never met, it was finally time for her to "come home."

As Bruce drove up to our home, I laughed to see a tall, lean dog in the passenger front seat. There she was – mysterious, breathtakingly beautiful, and humorous with such adorable large ears. I ran inside to get George, giddy with excitement over this new dog who had come so far.

I told him, "She is so cute, this has to work out."

Once Bruce and Roman exited the car, with Shayla on a soft leash, we greeted each other nervously. Roman spoke very limited English, but Bruce was able to interpret for us all. I think after Shayla's long journey, we were all praying and hoping that she would be a good fit with our family.

The rescue group's trainer arrived as George stepped out to join us. I knelt and reached my open hand out to Shayla, under her chin, and said hello. She looked at George and me with stunning golden eyes that just captured our hearts from that first day. So exotic and mysterious that we could sense her wolf spirit, yet so gentle and sweet. She was friendly and allowed us to pet her, but she was curious about the yard and ready to explore. Bruce said, "She has a hopeful, sweet disposition and positive outlook at all times, even as a stray. She is very smart." What a perfect description.

We walked her around the yard on leash, then brought Juneau out to meet her, also on leash. We were all amazed at how much they looked alike, despite an almost 10-year age difference. Both sporting black and tan fur, in almost the same body areas, Juneau's hair just a bit longer, and Shayla standing taller but leaner, they could have been cousins. George and I walked around our large field with the trainer, who kept Shayla on a controlled leash as Juneau ran alongside. The dogs seemed interested in each other and got along well together.

As we walked, the trainer pointed out a few things to watch for (like tree branches too close to the 5' chain link fence), warning us that Shayla's Czech wolfdog traits meant she could be curious, adventurous, and energetic. We thought she was exaggerating, but within the next couple of weeks, Shayla seemed to vanish from our yard a few times.

No, she did not climb up or over the fence or tree branches (but we cut them back anyway). This clever escape artist dug under the fence – the trainer didn't mention that possibility.

After our pack walk, we all went inside and showed Shayla her new home. Bruce read the "Welcome Home" sign to Roman, who smiled in agreement that this was a good home for his friend. Assured the dogs were fine together, and with George and I just awestruck by Shayla, we agreed we wanted her. We spoke a bit longer with Bruce and Roman, eager to learn every last bit of information about Shayla and her life. Then Bruce handed me Shayla's leash – she was officially our dog.

Before they left, I watched as Roman knelt beside Shayla, speaking to her in Ukrainian. Her face cupped in his hands, wiping away a tear as he kissed her good-bye. Obviously, he loved her and would miss her, but he seemed happy for her. His promise of a forever family was now fulfilled. She seemed to listen to every word Roman said to her, as they stared into each other's eyes in a private moment, just meant for those two souls to connect. What a kind and good-hearted Christian man. He knew that from that day forward, they would carry a piece of each other's heart, and that true friendship lasts forever. He also knew that God loved Shayla and would provide the best home for her. Bruce and Roman both hugged Shayla, then drove away.

We gently reassured Shayla, saying, "Welcome home sweetheart, we're so happy you are here. You will have a great life here."

I hoped that one day we would have that deep emotional connection with her, like Roman. I also wondered how Alina and Mykola must feel about Shayla being so far away. I hoped Roman would tell them that she found a good home.

Shayla left Ukraine a young dog, full of hope and promise, and arrived safely in America, with Roman's promise of a good new life about to start. It was time for her to pass from one set of loving caretakers to another, from one life to another. She crossed the invisible bridge between two worlds, from a lonely puppy and young adult to a forever home and her own family who truly wanted her. Over the years to come, as we hoped, trust and the emotional bond between the four of us grew. I never dreamed of the adventure that began for all of us that day she came to live with us.

We believe that although this was not the family or life that Shayla was born into, this was the family God meant for her to be with.

Crossing the Bridge - Ukraine to America

Chapter Nine:
Shayla's New Life

Well, I would like to say over the next couple of years that Shayla was always the good girl Roman told her to be – but that would not be the truth. She seemed content and happy to be with us, and loved having a human "Mom" and "Dad" to love her, along with her big brother Juneau to play with. But sometimes that old spirit of adventure overcame her, and she would dig under the fence to run through the neighboring open canyon. After all, there were more rabbits and lizards to chase! She could only get under the fence one way, not back under. George and I were not pleased when we had to go to the neighbor's property to get her back, but we were sure glad to get her home. That is one interesting way to get to know your neighbors better.

Sometimes we would take the dogs to the vet or groomer for nail trims. As soon as anyone even touched Shayla's nails, she howled like a banshee so that everyone in the shop knew she was there. Yes, I had to admit that drama queen was my dog, ugh, as I apologized to the staff and other customers. They just smiled.

Just a day after Shayla joined our family, Juneau was digging a hole in the dirt under the big tree where he liked to lay. Shayla decided she wanted to play too, so she ran up behind him and pounced on top of him, surprising him amid his important dig. Yay – how fun.

But Juneau just looked at Shayla as if to say, "Who are you and where the heck did you come from? Don't you know this is important?"

Nevertheless, Juneau and Shayla became good friends and learned to work together rather quickly. Juneau seemed content as his role changed from young hyper puppy under Honey's training, to the wise old teacher with this young pup Shayla. He taught her to grow up and mind what their human pack leaders told them. She learned that her new job was to be a faithful and fun companion for our family and help keep Juneau young in spirit. She also learned that by slowing down to walk at his pace, together they could find the most incredible smells in our yard and along the trails we walked. She followed him everywhere, respecting her elder's wise teachings. Age does not determine or limit the wisdom nor friendship of people, or animals. With friends of different ages (some older and some younger), cultures, and physical capabilities, my life (and Shayla's) expands in wonderful ways.

We make sure the dogs have everything necessary (good food, treats, comfy beds, affection, a safe home, okay also their own embroidered Christmas stockings), but Shayla does seem to miss interacting with children. She will never shy away from walking up to a child or teen to befriend them. She almost seems to smile and understand when someone walks by and tells her what a pretty girl she is. I love that Juneau and Shayla can make a sad person smile; a rushed person stop for a moment.

One day the four of us drove to Balboa Park, San Diego. After enjoying an outdoor concert, a lady with a young girl and boy came over to talk with us and meet the dogs. The kids sat down next to the dogs. Although they were strangers, Shayla rolled over onto her side, legs splayed in mid-air, smiling, and the children took turns scratching her tummy and petting Juneau's head. Perhaps for a moment, Shayla was back in Ukraine with her children. Kids were kids, no matter what country, and kids and dogs just share their special world where time stands still. Shayla loves making new friends, and even Juneau warmed up quickly, following Shayla's confident lead.

Chapter Ten:
Moving On Together

Shayla at Courthouse in Prescott, Arizona

Just when Shayla had learned a steady routine, and become accustomed to her new San Diego environment, I retired from the San Diego City Attorney's Office. After almost 30 years of knowing my place in the working world, my life completely changed in June 2021. Working as a City Attorney Senior Paralegal for the last couple of years had been a mixed blessing as I enjoyed leadership, training, and advocating for my staff, but first-line supervision is seldom easy. My emotions were mixed with pride in a job well done, sadness at leaving friends, and excitement for a future that would now be of my choosing. For the first time, I was able to contemplate a life outside of my hometown. My parents were gone, no kids, and George had been off work for a couple of months before my retirement, burdened with a significant shoulder injury that prevented him from resuming work as a landscaper. We were ready to embrace change. Ready to do something that would be fun, help others, and follow God's direction for the details. Months later, I experienced my first ziplining and a tethered free fall high rope called "leap of faith." The idea of jumping off a perfectly good platform into mid-air (especially the leap of faith with nothing to hold onto) requires focus, and a LOT of trust that God will hold and protect you. Kind of like packing up your life, moving to a new home where you don't know anyone, and starting a new life where God leads. Shayla did it, George and I did it, Roman and the orphanage did it. Let fear give way to trust as God is always faithful.

I previously visited with friends in Arizona, including a couple of trips to Prescott, and fell in love with "everybody's hometown." Other friends who recently moved to Arizona praised it as the place to go. Close enough to "home" (San Diego), the smaller mountain community with more affordable housing prices to fit our retirement budget, and the proximity of friends throughout Arizona, enticed our interest. We trusted God in this move and He blessed us with "plans to give us hope and a future" in a great new home. The property even included a woodworking shop so that George could fulfill his life-long passion to become a professional woodworker. Our new neighbors Deb and Craig were wonderful and so welcoming. It may not be the dog shelter property we originally wanted, but I found a great animal rescue group to volunteer with (United Animal Friends), as time permitted.

One day in September 2021, after selling our Lakeside home, we packed up the moving van headed for our new Prescott home. Juneau and Shayla surely must have wondered what was happening as strangers walked through our home and we started packing boxes. We even left for a few days to settle into our new home, with a caretaker to watch the dogs. I wondered if Shayla thought she was going to be abandoned or taken away again. Was it time to move on to a new life and family again? Yet Juneau was still with her in their same home. The dogs were so happy when George and I returned after a couple of days.

We finished packing and one early morning while it was still dark, the four of us piled into the car, together again, and moved on to a new home and a new world in Prescott, Arizona.

In this new life, George and I found more time to spend with our dogs and each day brought a new adventure. Mountain hikes, courthouse walks, and even kayaking on warm days. Now I work part-time again, as a paralegal for two wonderful attorneys, and enjoy volunteering with the dog rescue. But our dogs will always be a priority in my life. George is home with them some days, and we still enjoy our weekend outings and morning devotional walks together. I have enjoyed getting to know new friends in town while still treasuring friends in my hometown. Like Shayla, I have found that friends come in all ages, sizes, physical abilities. Count them all as blessings.

We needed a little time to get accustomed to the different environment and weather - summer monsoons with dark skies and thunder mixed with days of rain and snow. Shayla sometimes gets scared by the thunder and lightning but those are the times she lies cuddled up beside me, trusting that I will calm her world and keep her safe. Just as I trust that God will calm my world despite moments of chaos.

We found more time for a favorite activity of both dogs: learning a training routine. Previously, Juneau had completed obedience and even agility training. Our shy boy learned to run through a long-enclosed tunnel, walk across a board, and step through ladder rungs. Shayla was always up for a new adventure, and she learned these exercises quickly by watching Juneau. She also quickly learned our simple commands and how to respond consistently to *Sit, Down, Stay, Come,* and even weave between my legs for a treat. She enjoys training, waiting for the command, and trusting that every appropriate response will be rewarded with praise and treats, but she also seems truly pleased when she gets a command correct. I only wish I learned my lessons so quickly, to wait and trust patiently for God's next step when work is scarce, bills are looming, or some troubling situation arises.

We enrolled Shayla in a 6-week class led by an experienced trainer, Lisa Saputo. She is kind but firm, always encouraging the dogs while challenging them to learn more. Over the weeks Shayla proved to us, and Lisa, that she enjoyed the training and wanted to learn. She usually obeyed Lisa's commands promptly, watching every cue, even throwing herself into a *Down* position with such gusto as her legs and belly hit the ground. She seemed to think it was also her job to control the younger dogs in class, casting a disappointed glance or perhaps a slight growl to the overly hyper husky. Lisa taught Shayla (and us) even more fun and challenging things to do like *Wait, Cross Over* (to the other side of the sidewalk/street), and *Crawl.* Shayla passed the course and was able to take that champion graduate's walk around the Prescott courthouse with us, Lisa, and her dog Jackson. Lisa said Shayla was smart and learned quickly. As all of this training paid off in her regular obedience, our family became a "pack" partnership, bonded by mutual trust, which made all of our lives happier. It took time, but I believe we earned Shayla's trust, love, and thanks as she earned ours. We learned from each other. However, not chasing rabbits remains an eternal challenge for her!

Recently Shayla and I resumed training with Lisa, focusing on the 10 Steps towards Shayla's Canine Good Citizen designation. She passed the test the first time and is now CGC certified via the American Kennel Club.

Recently we met a wonderful woman, Cindy, entirely by chance (actually God's incredible timing and planning), who is involved with a Ukrainian community organization in our town. Shayla, George, her trainer Lisa, and I even got to participate in the Ukranian Festival fundraiser in Prescott. We share Shayla's incredible story with people as George displayed and sold some of his beautiful custom woodwork (Wathen Custom Woodcrafts). Shayla our Vlcak even sported a festive Ukrainian vinok collar, she would have made Ukraine proud.

As people walked by and spoke to her in Ukranian, she would tilt her head as if to say "I remember that language and my friends in my first home."

I am also learning that to proceed with training her to be an even better dog, I must begin to "discipline" Shayla by withholding certain privileges. She now travels in the back seat of our car, not in the front. She now waits to be invited to sit with me on the couch as a special reward. And she's doing just fine, the change was tougher on me.

But now I understand why even the American Kennel Club stated, "The Czechoslovakian Vlcak is not recommended for first-time owners as they need strong pack leadership and structure."

I had to truly be her pack leader, to treat her like a regular dog, rather than a princess or an animal to be pitied for a tough puppyhood. Only then could I view her as my canine teammate, capable together of perhaps helping others. I want her to remain calm in a sit or down position when meeting people, yet share her exuberant joy of life to encourage others.

She has so much more to offer people rather than just being a silly spoiled puppy. I stop and think how much I need to mature and allow God to be my "pack leader" rather than running about, half-crazed with a busy schedule, worried about life. If He disciplines me or strives to teach me something, it does not mean that He doesn't love me, just that He wants me to grow stronger by following Him.

Forever Friends – Shayla and Juneau

Chapter Eleven:
Shayla's Future Plans

    I would like to train Shayla as a therapy dog, now that she is CGC certified. She loves children so much that I see a dog who endured tough times and can now help people (young and old) find a way to endure and create a happier life. Whether that be helping children who were adopted or grew up in a tough situation (like Shayla) or domestic violence (like Juneau), or just shy and insecure (like me) in a tough world.

Unfortunately, I have not been able to find a group yet that will accept Shepherd/wolfdog mixes, even ones that grew up in an orphanage loving kids. But I won't give up yet; Shayla would not give up, and she is so worth it!

Since Shayla loves adventure, and we love kayaking, we hope that one day we can take Shayla out on a boat. Perhaps she will learn to dive into one of the beautiful lakes here in Prescott on a warm summer day?

Shayla is a very smart, happy, and loving dog, content to be a cherished family member. She is blessed by God through His love and the friends she has met so far through this sometimes-tough journey and adventure of life. Shayla is forever a blend of proud instinct shepherd/wolfdog, the bravery of Mykola to overcome hardship, the love of the orphaned children she touched, the faith of Roman to trust God, the kindness of Alina and the Korniyko family and Bruce, and the strength of her home country Ukraine. Add to that the wisdom of her "big brother" Juneau, George's courage to overcome tough situations, and hopefully compassion from me. She makes the world a happier and friendlier place everywhere she goes, something we can all strive to achieve.

Epilogue
Follow Up With Father's House

Simba & Nala (The Saved & The Lost)

We were so deeply touched by Roman and Bruce that we came to truly care about the people at Father's House and Ukraine, a country and culture so far away, one that we never knew about. It has been my honor to stay in touch with the Korniykos and Bruce, as friends, to follow their journey as refugees to Germany when the war in Ukraine broke out, and to pray for their safety. They inspired me to tell their story, and Shayla's, to share their blessing and hopefully inspire others. Don't ever give up!

Early in 2022, Russian soldiers invaded Ukraine, eventually moving on to Kiev near Otchiy Dim. As news of impending invasion became more real, Roman started preparing for the worst-case scenario. On the day the war broke out, though, all his plans seemed to fall apart. The buses he had planned on to evacuate the children and staff were all canceled. As he heard missile strikes all around their village of Petrivske, the staff moved the children to the bomb shelter. Roman's faith in God remained the only steadfast thing in his life. He prayed for protection and God provided a miracle.

He received a phone call from a Ukrainian stranger. The man said, "If you are ready in 3 hours, I will take your kids to the Ukrainian border."

With no time to spare, Roman obtained government help to obtain passports, readied a couple of minibuses on site, and mobilized the staff and children. They asked the children and adults not to eat anything as they would not be able to stop for the bathroom. Everyone, even the youngest children, understood and agreed, without crying or complaining, just praying. The man proved good on his word and arrived with two large buses, driving one of the buses himself. He even arranged for a police escort to the Polish border.

The orphanage's leaders, staff, and almost 150 children (orphans and children of staff) were forced to quickly depart their beloved home that February night, taking few belongings and not knowing if or when they would return. Young children who had already lost so much through trauma, family betrayal, and abandonment, were now forced to move on again.

Police officers escorted the buses through crowded roads and highways, despite reports of the planned bombing.

Roman believes it was God's miracle they made it safely to Ukraine's border: "Angels guided us and made an open way for us."

When they were a few hours away from the border crossing, near Rivne, believing they were safe, the entourage stopped at a gas station so the kids could use the bathroom. Within 5 minutes of exiting the buses though, they started hearing constant bomb strikes and shelling all around them. Later they learned that was the airstrikes bombing the Rivne airport. Their brave police officer escorts hid the children with their bodies, hands touching to provide cover over their heads as hovering angels as the kids ran to the bathroom and back to the buses.

With the kids safely back on board the buses, the police directed Roman and the bus drivers to turn off all lights, keep silent, and follow the officers at top speed through the dark night. The children lay on the floor, hands over their heads, not making a sound. The police escorts turned on their emergency lights and sirens to direct the buses where to go, focusing any shelling or bombing attention on themselves and away from the buses. Roman described these brave officers who risked their lives to protect the children as their angels, sent by God.

Once they reached the Polish border, the police returned to Ukraine. Before they left, they told the children not to be afraid or sad but to go with God: "Go in peace and come back in peace. Believe that with God's help we will do all we can to protect our Ukraine so that you can return to your home in peace." Their venture was a miracle, blessed by God's loving protection. It took 12 hours to cross the border into Poland, but all were safe.

Days later, they arrived in Friedburg, Germany. A partnering nonprofit of Father's House had made living arrangements for them. The community and even the town's Mayor welcomed the children, provided food and medical care as needed, and showed them to the initial shelter barracks. Many children were traumatized by the evacuation and journey but gradually began to recover in their safe new country.

Roman initially had to leave his wife and daughters Alina and Anastasia behind at Father's House. The ladies stayed at the orphanage, with the two remaining dogs, a brother and sister pair of sweet Shepherds – Simba and Nala. Sadly, the female dog Nala strayed away from home and, despite Alina and Anastasia's days of search, was never found. Hopefully, she joined the stray animals still in Ukraine, rescued by animal organizations and good citizens. After a couple of weeks, the women were able to leave, with the remaining dog Simba, and safely drive to the border. They reunited with Roman and the children, and Simba was adopted by a loving forever family in Germany.

The leaders and children now live safely as refugees near Friedburg, Germany, praying for the day that they can return home to their beloved homeland in peace. Bruce Elliott and the Ambassadors of Father's House (the United States liaison for Father's House) continue to support and aid this orphanage. The leaders were unable to find one home large enough to accommodate everyone, but they have secured three family homes to move kids and foster parents to in family groups (each group has a "mom" and "dad"). Gradually lives are restored in part to a new normal, and children's activities like singing, theater groups, and arts and crafts have resumed. First graders are now attending German schools, learning German, while older kids resume Ukrainian school online. Roman helps the children give back to the Friedburg community that helped them by doing community cleanups and projects. He wants them to leave a positive impact and make a difference in the lives of the Friedburg people, to spread God's love.

Roman admits it is very difficult to be refugees in a new land where they must depend on others, and to leave their ministry, home, and beloved country. He wanted to remain in Ukraine or return to Ukraine once the children were safe in Germany, but he realizes his presence with them is more important for their stability. Anastasia has now returned to Ukraine. It is so difficult to comprehend why the Russians have destroyed their country.

Roman said, "Compared to Russia, Ukraine is such a small country, but David was also small and he was victorious over Goliath because God was with David. I want Ukraine to trust not in its strength, but to trust in the strength of God. Ukraine will stand and we will return home."

His prayer is for the healing and protection of these orphans, for loving families for each child, and for protection for Ukraine. My heart aches for Roman, his family, those at Father's House, the Ukrainian refugees, and those who remain in Ukraine (people and animals), as well as for the Russian civilians who also had to flee their country.

Meanwhile, back at Otchiy Dim, some of the men who helped maintain the orphanage in Ukraine and work with the children remain. They provide community service aid, food, and temporary shelter for homeless Ukrainian citizens passing along en route to new homes. A few of these brave men have joined the Ukrainian resistance army, fighting for their beloved homeland. Meanwhile, the children and staff in Germany host fundraisers to send supplies back to their friends at Father's House. In September Father's House in Ukraine was preparing for 36 new war orphans to move in, meeting a new and desperate need. They are always praying for peace.

Following the current events of Ukraine, and Father's House in particular, reminds us that we are all united in spirit through God's love. As casualties continue to rise, statistics increase on the billions of dollars of infrastructure damage, stories are told of horrendous war crimes committed, innocent people and pets are killed in the streets of Ukraine, it sometimes seems so difficult to keep faith in God. Yet, as Roman said, Ukraine will stand and the people will return to their beloved homeland. Till then, we join Roman and the brave Ukrainian people with our prayers for peace.

Bruce has informed me that unfortunately, America's Center for Disease Control (CDC) has now banned future dog rescues from Ukraine, based on bad breeders and veterinarians falsifying rabies certificates. Sad as he wanted to bring more dogs here. Fortunately, Shayla came to America when she did.

Acknowledgments

My sincere gratitude and appreciation to my publisher/editor Lizzy McNett (Writers Publishing House) for her support, encouragement, and belief in me that this was a good story that needed to be told.

I thank the Korniyko family, Mykola, and Bruce Elliott for sharing your story and Shayla's story with me and entrusting us to be the forever home for your special dog.

I express my sincere appreciation for my husband George, whose constant encouragement was a tremendous support in writing this story. You accepted and embraced my love for dogs through muddy paws, dog hair, and all to make our family complete.

I am forever grateful to my parents Herbert and Shirlee Bolger who taught me such a deep love of animals, and provided a stable and loving childhood home and family.

My thanks to many wonderful friends (Kathy, Debbie, Lisa, Lucien, Mary, Kristie, Cassie, Steve, Lynn, and others) who taught, supported, encouraged, and believed I could do this, even when I doubted. So glad to share this journey of life with you as friends, and fellow dog lovers.

Thanks to author Jeri K. Tory Conklin who took the time to learn from Shayla and Juneau of their life journeys.

I dedicate this story to my sweet Shayla and gentle Juneau (and our former incredible canine companions Riley, Honey, and Blaze) who taught me that patience, living in the moment, acceptance, gratitude, overcoming fears, faith, love, and most of all treating everyone as a friend makes life so much richer. I appreciate how the homebody guys (George and Juneau) have supported us adventurous gals (Shayla and I) and given us wings to fly.

Most of all, I thank God for inspiring this story of how loving a Father can be and blessing my life with these amazing human and canine friends. I am so thankful that You have loved me so faithfully, even when my dogs remember Your teachings much better than I do.

Author's Bio

Barchelle ("Chelly") Bolger Wathen, a native San Diegan, now resides in Prescott, Arizona. She loves spending time with her husband, George, and their two "fur kids" Juneau and Shayla. She is a college graduate with a Master of Public Administration degree, and worked almost thirty years as a paralegal/senior paralegal with the San Diego City Attorney's Office. From legal documents and grant proposals to college papers and her thesis, Chelly always enjoyed writing.

"Shayla & Friends" is Chelly's first non-fiction published work. A true story about her remarkable, adventurous dog Shayla who came to America from a Ukrainian orphanage, and the friends she made along the way.

Chelly still works as a paralegal for two Prescott attorneys, but also enjoys volunteering with local animal rescue groups. But her favorite activity is enjoying God's creation with family and friends - kayaking, ziplining, and hiking mountain trails, especially with Shayla.

Other works by Barchelle:

You may continue to follow Shayla and Friends' adventures on her Instagram page: @juneaushayla and her website at shaylaandfriends.com.

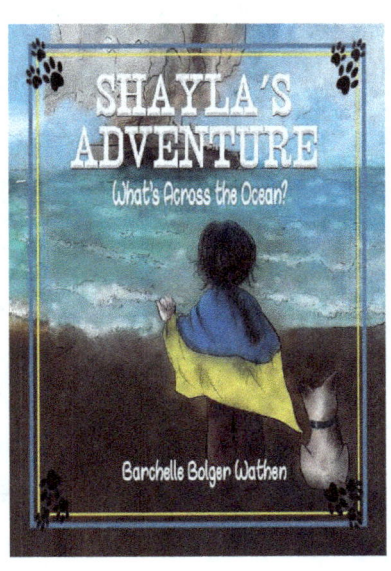

A portion of proceeds from this book and the children's book "Shayla's Adventure – What's Across the Ocean?" will go to benefit Ambassadors of Father's House orphanage (www.a-fh.org) to provide for these young lives, and recognized shelters working to rescue abandoned Ukrainian animals. Donations are gratefully appreciated.

References

America, T. C. (n.d.). Retrieved from https://czechoslovakianvlcak.org/#team-7

Club, A. K. (n.d.). *Czechoslovakian Vlcak Dog Breed Information - American Kennel Club (akc.org).* Retrieved from https://www.akc.org/dog-breeds/czechoslovakian-vlcak/